Operation Barbarossa

A Captivating Guide to the Opening Months of the War between Hitler and the Soviet Union in 1941–45

© Copyright 2020

All Rights Reserved. No part of this book may be reproduced in any form without permission in writing from the author. Reviewers may quote brief passages in reviews.

Disclaimer: No part of this publication may be reproduced or transmitted in any form or by any means, mechanical or electronic, including photocopying or recording, or by any information storage and retrieval system, or transmitted by email without permission in writing from the publisher.

While all attempts have been made to verify the information provided in this publication, neither the author nor the publisher assumes any responsibility for errors, omissions or contrary interpretations of the subject matter herein.

This book is for entertainment purposes only. The views expressed are those of the author alone, and should not be taken as expert instruction or commands. The reader is responsible for his or her own actions.

Adherence to all applicable laws and regulations, including international, federal, state and local laws governing professional licensing, business practices, advertising and all other aspects of doing business in the US, Canada, UK or any other jurisdiction is the sole responsibility of the purchaser or reader.

Neither the author nor the publisher assumes any responsibility or liability whatsoever on the behalf of the purchaser or reader of these materials. Any perceived slight of any individual or organization is purely unintentional.

Free Bonus from Captivating History (Available for a Limited time)

Hi History Lovers!

Now you have a chance to join our exclusive history list so you can get your first history ebook for free as well as discounts and a potential to get more history books for free! Simply visit the link below to join.

Captivatinghistory.com/ebook

Also, make sure to follow us on Facebook, Twitter and Youtube by searching for Captivating History.

Contents

FREE BONUS FROM CAPTIVATING HISTORY (AVAILABLE FOR A LIMITED TIME) 1
INTRODUCTION 3
CHAPTER 1 – NAZIS AND COMMUNISTS 5
CHAPTER 2 – INVASION 28
CHAPTER 3 – ALL SEEMS LOST 36
CONCLUSION 46
BIBLIOGRAPHY 47

Introduction

On June 22nd, 1941, Nazi Germany launched Operation Barbarossa, the invasion of the Soviet Union. In the time since the end of the war, the world has become familiar with the number of deaths sustained by the Soviet Union (also known as the USSR) during the conflict—twenty-million. And that's likely low, given the size of the country, census taking at the time, and the damage done to the bureaucracy of the country. Think about it: twenty million people. That is a figure that is almost impossible to wrap one's mind around. Nearly every family in the nation lost someone. The most celebrated and biggest holiday in the Soviet Union, now the nations of Russia, Ukraine, and Belarus (the former Soviet republics that were most affected by the war) is May 8th, "Victory Day, " which celebrates the USSR's victory over Nazi Germany in what was called the Great Patriotic War, honoring the heroes and remembering those lost.

Geoffrey Roberts, a British historian of the Soviet Union in World War II, in his work, *Stalin's Wars: From World War to Cold War, 1939-1953* (2006), attempted to tally the losses in terms of infrastructure, making them all the starker. During the Nazi invasion and occupation, the Soviet Union lost an estimated:

70,000 Soviet cities, towns, and villages

32,000 factories

6,000 hospitals
82,000 schools
43,000 libraries

Historian Jacob Pauwels and others found that the USSR did not regain its pre-war economic levels until the early/mid-1960s.

Adolf Hitler invaded the Soviet Union with over three million men. The Soviets had just under that number in the western section of their country to meet them, as well as millions more elsewhere, which was something Hitler did not count on and grossly underestimated.

The struggle between the Soviet Union and Nazi Germany was one of the largest and deadliest conflicts of all time, a war of elimination between totalitarian nations led by two of the most ruthless leaders in the history of the world.

Chapter 1 – Nazis and Communists

In *Mein Kampf* (*My Struggle*), Hitler's political testament and "autobiography" (in quotes because much of what is written about his life was exaggerated or made up, especially his claim of poverty; his father was a big fish in a small town with a maid, a pension, a uniform, and respect), the future dictator of Germany repeatedly stated his belief that it was the destiny of the German nation to expand to the east.

Germany, after World War I and even today, is roughly the size of the American states of Washington and Oregon together. The population of those two states combined is about twelve million people. The population of Germany at the time of World War II was seventy million (today, it's eighty million). Hitler was not the only German-speaking person to hold the belief that Germany needed to secure *Lebensraum* ("living space") in order to thrive and survive in a crowded Europe with enemies on all sides. Indeed, along with the vicious anti-Semitism included within *Mein Kampf,* the idea of *Lebensraum* is the most mentioned and elaborated upon.

In the years before the war, many of those in other nations who had read Hitler's book and who saw him clearly for what he was repeatedly told anyone who was willing to listen that Hitler meant to start a war of expansion in the east, which might evolve into another world war. Chief among these people was one of the leading political figures of Great Britain and its future leader, Winston Churchill.

In the years before the previous world war, many Europeans (especially those in the larger and more powerful nations of France, the United Kingdom, Austria-Hungary, Germany, and Russia) held the belief that their nations needed to gain or hold onto territories and colonial empires in order to thrive. Though much of this late 19th-century imperialism was supported by an undercurrent of racial superiority, its aims were economic gains and the power and prestige that came with a large empire.

However, Germany, prior to World War I, had a sizable minority of politicians, writers, philosophers, and journalists who were beginning to gravitate to a vision of Germany and Germanic peoples (which included the British, Scandinavians, Dutch, etc.) as a "superior" race, noting both their economic and military power along with their outsized cultural influence. This "Germanic superiority" extended over the other peoples of Europe, especially to the Slavic nations of the east.

Hitler, along with many Germans, Austrians, and other Europeans, were not alone in holding these beliefs; they existed in the United States and Canada as well. In the years between World War I and World War II, these ideas combined with new advances in science to bring forth the new "science" of eugenics, the idea that it would be possible to medically weed out hereditary and other infirmities such as intellectual disabilities, epilepsy, alcoholism, etc. On its fringes, the field of eugenics included educated medical professionals and philosophers who believed that it would be possible to "breed out" such infirmities and encourage the procreation of individuals who were believed to be smarter, better-looking, more fit, and healthy. Once it was combined with the idea that Northern European Germanic peoples were superior, eugenics began to enter a new and dangerous phase by the time Hitler came to power.

(It should be noted that in the 1920s and even after World War II, the United States, Canada, and Sweden carried out forced sterilizations of people deemed "undesirable." This began before Hitler took power in Germany and continued after his defeat.)

Additionally, in much of Europe (actually more so in Eastern Europe and Russia than in the West at this time), this idea of racial superiority combined with anti-Semitism, which had been the scourge of the Jewish population ever since the Romans forced the Jews from Israel centuries before, formed a dangerous new set of ideas, including the idea that a "master race" could be bred and "inferior" races could be eliminated.

The cataclysmic event that pushed many Germans and Austrians, where anti-Semitism, including obviously that of Hitler, was particularly virulent, was World War I. The German defeat in World War I shocked the population, and it deserves some attention because it foretold what was to come—especially its severity.

There were many factors leading to Germany's defeat in the First World War. Among them was the power of the nations arrayed against them: France, Great Britain, Russia, Italy, and, from 1917, on, the United States.

Germany and, to a lesser extent Austria, its ally, were able to keep their enemies from actually invading their territory at the end of the war, but those in Germany with an intimate knowledge of the situation knew that it was just a matter of time before that happened. Their enemies were too powerful, and with the entry of the US into the war, the Allies were just getting more powerful by the week.

The two men in charge of the German war efforts in 1918 were Field Marshals Paul von Hindenburg and Erich Ludendorff. Knowing that the war was lost, they purposely approached the leading opposition party in Germany, the Social Democratic Party (a democratic party with some socialist aspects to their platform) about going to the Allies to negotiate a peace. They knew that the Allies would not accept a peace offer from the German military but that they would from known opponents of the war.

This was partially true, but the field marshals' main motive was to take the onus of defeat/surrender off of the Imperial German Army and onto the politicians, especially left-wing politicians. In this, they succeeded. The Social Democratic diplomats negotiated with the Allies for a truce, which eventually, and unavoidably, turned into a German surrender.

Another factor that caused such a major shock to much of German society was that throughout the war, and to some extent before, the German press was tightly controlled by the government. Simply speaking, in the papers for every day for four years, the German populace was told they were winning the war and that victory was "just around the corner." This was especially true in the spring of 1918 when Field Marshal Ludendorff launched his Spring Offensive, which was designed to knock France and Britain out of the war before the full weight of American manpower and resources could be brought to bear on Germany.

At first, the Germans enjoyed spectacular successes, but eventually, the power of the Allies began to push the Germans back. Though no Allied troops were in Germany by the time the war ended on November 11th, 1918, the German Army was just days away from a full retreat—supplies were low, replacements were barely trained boys, and the number of those were quickly dwindling.

Though many Germans realized the situation was dire, many chose to keep their rose-colored glasses on and believe that victory was still near. Then, suddenly, Germany surrendered.

By the time the Treaty of Versailles was signed the next summer, a story had already begun that the German Army had been "stabbed in the back" by enemies from within. Among those "enemies" were already unpopular groups, such as the communists and the Jewish and, to a lesser extent, left-leaning people in other parties, mainly the Social Democrats.

Under the Treaty of Versailles, the German armed forces, one of the pillars of German society, was limited to 100,000 men. Millions of men were no longer allowed to pursue a military career.

Germany was also forced to cede the long-disputed territory of Alsace-Lorraine to France and to give up the territory it had won in Russia. Making it worse, the "new" country of Poland, long divided by Germany, Russia, and Austria-Hungary, was born, and it took up much of what used to be German territory, actually separating the state of Prussia from the rest of the country.

On top of all this, the Germans were also required to pay a huge amount in reparations to the Allies and, to add insult to injury, accept the blame for starting the war, which was not entirely true. As you might imagine, all of this gave birth to much resentment (actually, resentment might be too mild), which only grew with time. Not to mention, it was aggravated by the economic hardships of the post-war period, which included the onset of the Great Depression in 1929.

Throughout all of this, Hitler's *Nationalsozialistische Deutsche Arbeiterpartei* (National Socialist German Workers' Party, better known as the Nazi Party, called this for the pronunciation of the first part of the first word in German) waxed and waned in influence and power. As Germany's economic situation worsened during the Great Depression, more and more people began to join the party, literally and tacitly. Throughout the late 1920s and early 1930s, the resentments in Germany grew, and the blame for Germany's problems was placed squarely on the Jews and the communists.

Many of Europe's and the world's communist parties were controlled, or at least influenced, by Stalin's Soviet Union.

Josef Stalin certainly did try to destabilize the governments and societies of Europe in the hope that the uncertain economic times of the immediate post-war years, as well as during the Great Depression in 1929, would encourage the workers and peasants of Europe to unite and overthrow the capitalist systems in place there. Of course, if that happened, Stalin fully intended to play the role of a puppet master.

By the late 1920s, Stalin had risen to completely control the Soviet Union. He used political favors, threats, and incredible repression (executions, forced labor, labor camps, etc.) to maintain this power.

And though the statistics coming out of the Soviet Union were greatly inflated, by the time World War II began, he had turned the Soviet Union into an industrial powerhouse. He also built the Soviet Union's Red Army into one of the largest fighting forces on the planet.

In early 1933, Hitler came to power in Germany and launched a bold yet careful plan to both regain Germany's lost territories and rearm the armed forces, which would violate the Treaty of Versailles. One of his first orders of business was to outlaw all opposition parties and to jail or execute the members of the Communist Party of Germany, the largest communist party outside of the USSR at the time.

Ironically, while he was doing this, Hitler was also reaching agreements with Stalin and the Soviets to secretly train elements of the future German armed forces in the Soviet Union. This had begun in secret by the German military before Hitler, but he continued it and enlarged the program, obviously with the agreement of Stalin.

Despite being ideological enemies, both Hitler and Stalin were pragmatists. Hitler supplied machine parts and other goods to Stalin, and in return, he got a place to rebuild the German military in secret. Stalin aimed to set in play a series of machinations that would turn Hitler against France and Britain rather than his country, which would allow the USSR to build an army with which to defend itself from a resurgent Germany. Stalin, for the most part, believed that Germany and the Soviet Union would war against each other; he just hoped he could control the timing of the conflict.

Hitler began his program to reassert Germany's power in 1936. First, he remilitarized the Rhineland. He then annexed Austria in 1938. Later that year and at the start of 1939, he manipulated the French and British into abandoning Czechoslovakia in the interests of peace and took over that nation as well. He formed alliances with Hungary and Romania, as well as Benito Mussolini's Italy and Emperor Hirohito's Japan. Soon, Stalin realized that Hitler and his allies had him surrounded.

When Hitler threatened and cajoled the Western Allies over Czechoslovakia, Stalin was actually willing to face down Germany, but only if Britain and France showed some resolve. When they did not, he came to believe that not only would they not be able to withstand Hitler but that he had also better come to terms with the Nazi leader before it was too late.

As Germany put pressure on Poland, which was step one in Hitler's desire to expand eastward, the Soviets and Germans began putting out diplomatic feelers. Hitler wanted to invade Poland without provoking a war with the USSR, as he did not believe Germany was ready to take on the Soviet Union. Stalin wanted to reassert Russian control over Poland and to gain a buffer zone between himself and Hitler.

An agreement was beneficial for both, so on August 23rd, 1939, the two totalitarian powers signed a non-aggression pact. The Molotov-Ribbentrop Pact (named after the foreign ministers of the USSR and Germany, respectively) openly declared that Hitler and Stalin would not go to war with each other. It also announced a variety of trade agreements and diplomatic protocols. Those were just the open announcements. Secretly, Stalin and Hitler agreed to divide Poland between them as Germany (or rather, the German-speaking state of Prussia) and Russia had for centuries. It also gave Stalin a free hand to take control of the Baltic states and part of Romania, and the pact assured Stalin that Hitler would not interfere if the USSR attacked Finland, with whom Stalin was having border issues.

On the surface, it seemed as if Stalin got the better of the bargain, but what Hitler really wanted was a large chunk of Poland and an assurance that the Soviet Union would not attack him when he turned to wage war on France, the planning of which was already in the works.

Hitler attacked Poland on September 1st, 1939. Within four weeks, the Germans were in the Polish capital of Warsaw. Stalin sent in the Red Army on September 17th. By the end of the month, Poland ceased to exist, and the German and Soviet troops made big shows of congratulating each other all along the agreed stopping line. Very quickly, German machine parts and industrial goods started traveling east as Russian raw materials flowed into Germany.

Illustration 1: German and Soviet officers meet in Poland, September 1939

In November, Stalin ordered the Red Army to attack Finland. He wanted a greater buffer between the Finnish border and the Soviet's "second city" and home of the Bolshevik Revolution, Leningrad (today's St. Petersburg). Stalin was worried that at some point in the future, Hitler would ally himself with the Finns, who had a long history of antagonism toward the Russians.

Though Stalin eventually got what he wanted, as the Finns were forced to cede substantial chunks of territory to the Soviets, the Red Army's campaign in Finland, though short, was costly in both money and human life. Eventually, the Soviets' weight of numbers showed through, but the Finns had outfought the Red Army at nearly every turn until they became too exhausted and were forced into negotiations.

The Red Army Purges of the 1930s

The common belief is that Hitler and many others saw the Red Army as incompetent in their Finnish campaign. This is true, to a large extent, and it helped Hitler reach his decision to invade the

USSR in 1941. However, many in Germany and around the world saw only what they wanted to see—a brutish and poorly led Red Army that relied on numbers to win. However, toward the end of the Winter War against the Finns, the Soviets stopped and reorganized, retrained, and replaced incompetent leaders with, for the most part, more able ones. This ability to bend and not break, along with surprising adaptability, would happen in the latter part of the Soviets' war with Hitler. But though the Soviets were able to reorganize enough to defeat Finland, their forces still suffered from some glaring weaknesses.

First and foremost, in the beginning of 1937, Stalin began a series of purges in order to solidify his already immense power. Though many segments of Soviet society suffered, it is the purge of the Red Army that concerns us here.

There is a debate among historians about why Stalin began the purges. Some believe it was simply his paranoia, for if a threat to his power arose (which there is no evidence there was), it would be among the officers of the Red Army. Others believe that Stalin and those close to him thought that many of the officers of the Red Army, particularly those who were promoted after the Bolshevik Revolution, were not as dedicated to communist ideals as they should have been. Among the party leadership, there was the belief that the armed forces did not need to spend much money on training a ton of officers, as "revolutionary zeal" would carry the day on the battlefield.

The man in charge of the Red Army in 1937 was the popular Mikhail Tukhachevsky, who led troops in the Bolshevik Revolution and the Russian Civil War and who was attempting to modernize the Red Army to bring it in line with modern ideas. Some believe that Stalin was jealous of Tukhachevsky's popularity and wished to eliminate him and his allies as they were possible rivals.

In 1937, Stalin's purge of the Red Army began. Of 80,000 officers, 37,000 were either killed outright, sent to Siberian labor camps to die, or jailed. Only a small number survived; some were later reinstated when it became clear to Stalin that experienced officers were needed to deal with Hitler's invasion. The numbers of causalities vary, as records were destroyed, altered, or hidden by the regime during the war as well as afterward, making it difficult to get exact numbers.

The purge was worse at the top, but it made its way down into the company level. At the top, three of the five Marshals of the Soviet Union were executed. And the list goes on: thirteen of fifteen generals of the army, eight of nine admirals, nearly 90 percent of corps commanders, 82 percent of all the division generals—and this was just at the top. Colonels, majors, and captains were removed as well, though at a lesser rate.

Making things worse was Stalin's purge of the political commissars attached to the armed forces. Even before the purge, the commissars made the efficient functioning of a modern army almost impossible. Down to the company level, commanders had a political shadow making sure that their commands were sufficiently in line with the ideas of the Communist Party. This meant time set aside for important training had to be used for indoctrinating men in Stalinist thought and communist teachings. The commissars also ensured that commanders followed orders, especially those given that included mass charges or other suicidal tactics in the belief that "zeal" would win the day. Officers who made a regular habit of opposing their commissars ran the risk of discipline, dismissal, or death.

In order to ensure complete loyalty among future commissars, from 1937 to 1938, the top echelon of political commissars (those attached to the staffs of marshals and generals) were eliminated. As in the rest of the army, these eliminations or dismissals usually meant a slow death in the Gulag, the Soviet system of labor/concentration camps.

By 1939, when the Molotov-Ribbentrop Pact was signed, the vast majority of the officers in the Red Army did not dare waver from the instructions given from the top. In the event that no instructions were given, the officers did not dare take matters into their own hands and figure out what was best to do—they were paralyzed with fear.

Stalin may have begun to realize the damage these purges had wrought when the Red Army suffered humiliation after humiliation in the war against Finland. Despite a three to one advantage in troops (the Red Army in total outnumbered the Finns by ten to one or more), the Finns lacking any serious heavy artillery, and the Soviets' possession of thousands of tanks to the Finns' mere 32, the Red Army struggled, in part because of its reliance on throwing wave after wave of men at the Finns with little regard to casualties.

As was mentioned earlier, Stalin and his generals finally realized things needed to change, and in the last month of the war, training and new tactics allowed the Soviets to advance and force the Finns to the negotiating table.

The German Army's Flexibility

In contrast to the Soviet system, the German Army under Hitler was surprisingly flexible. Before the unification of Germany, the people of the various German-speaking states all had their own military forces, but the most powerful was that of Prussia, the eastern German state, which became the core around which the German Empire was built in 1871.

The Prussian military, though small, was one of the first modern standing professional armies. Most other European nations had a small cadre of officers and a national guard, which often doubled as a police force. However, in times of war, troops had to be drafted, organized, and trained. More often than not, they were given far less training than was needed.

By contrast, beginning in the early 18th century, the Prussian kings organized a professional army whose sole purpose was the defense of the realm. Though comparatively small, the Prussians rotated men in and out of the army, so even those not officially in the ranks had enough training to act on the battlefield if the need arose immediately. This meant that, generally speaking, the Prussian Army was able to ready itself and move to attack or defend itself much quicker than its rivals. This system remained in place when Germany was born in 1871.

Prussian, and later German, training was notoriously strict and difficult, and though recruits were trained to obey orders instantly, there was also a kind of flexibility inherent in the Prussian/German system that was not present in other nations. The top of the chain of command set goals and timetables, but as orders filtered through the system, each successive group of commanders was allowed to act with flexibility in order to achieve those goals.

So, for example, the field marshals at the top might decide when an offensive would begin, its force allocation, timetable, general movements of armies, and their respective objectives/responsibilities. Down the ladder, army group commanders and the armies and divisions within that group would be given assignments, but it was up to the commanders as to how they would achieve their goals. This held true down to the company, platoon, and even the squad level on occasion. Adding to this flexibility, which allowed innovative techniques to be discovered much more often than in other armies, was the idea that each officer below trained for the job above him. So, division commanders trained as army commanders, regimental commanders as division command, etc. Even sergeants were familiar with the job of lieutenant. This meant that if the officer above them fell, the non-commissioned officer could be quickly promoted, allowing the battle to move forward without as many complications.

Ironically, during the course of World War II, as the tides of war turned, it was the Germans who became less flexible (at least on a divisional level and up) and the Soviets who became more flexible and innovative.

Balance of Forces

In 1942, Adolf Hitler was secretly recorded in a conversation with Finnish Field Marshal Carl Gustaf Emil Mannerheim. The two had met for Mannerheim's birthday and to discuss the progress of the war, which Finland had entered into on the side of Germany in 1941. In a surprisingly candid and conversational way, Hitler talks about the results of Operation Barbarossa, telling Mannerheim that he and his intelligence apparatus had grossly underestimated the size of the

Soviet armed forces and the industrial might that had helped to create it.

Sitting in a train car in Finland, Hitler told Mannerheim that, among other things, "If someone had told me that a country could start with 35,000 tanks, then I'd have said, 'You are crazy!' If one of my generals had stated that any nation had 35,000 tanks, I'd have said: 'You, my good sir, you see everything twice or ten times. You are crazy, you are seeing ghosts.'"

Hitler also goes on to admit that his army was not built for winter and that he had pinned his hopes on a swift victory. Despite all of this, though, Hitler goes on to say that even if he had known about the size of the Red Army and its industrial base, he would have attacked anyway based on how the Red Army performed in the Winter War with Finland and on his belief that he would eventually be involved in a war with the USSR, a war in which he wished to strike first.

What Hitler did not know was the extent of Soviet military spending. Though the USSR was poor compared to the richer Western European countries, throughout the late 1920s and 1930s, it had spent an increasing share of its national budget on defense. From 1927 to 1928, Stalin had spent about 10 percent of the nation's budget on the military. This percentage increased every year until the outbreak of the war, which first started with Finland in 1939. For comparison, in 1933, the Soviets spent 16 percent on defense spending; in 1938, it amounted to over 43 percent of the budget.

What follows is a basic and general run-down of the balance of forces for the Soviets and the Wehrmacht (German Armed Forces) when Operation Barbarossa started on June 22nd, 1941, on the Soviet border.

On the 1,800-mile-long border, Hitler had 153 (+/-5) divisions equaling 3.5 million men. In addition to those men were nineteen Panzer (tank) divisions, numbering around 6,000 tanks and other armored vehicles. Seven thousand artillery pieces of varying sizes thundered over the landscape that morning, along with over 7,000 mortars of varying sizes. These were accompanied by 3,000 to 5,000 aircraft. The German force was supplemented by thirty or so Finnish, Italian, Romanian, and Hungarian formations, totaling about thirty divisions of widely varied strength and effectiveness. This was the largest invasion force in world history—that is until the Soviets went on the offensive in late 1942/early 1943.

Opposing the Germans was a huge mass of Soviet infantry, but their effectiveness varied widely. The Soviets had approximately 2.5 to 2.9 million men on the front lines that morning and in the coming days. The Soviets had 11,000 tanks in the western part of the country and in Poland, outnumbering the Germans about two or three to one, depending on the sources of information. Airplanes, including fighters, bombers, recon, and transport, numbered between 8,000 to10,000, but these were largely obsolete. The Soviets possessed an amazing array of artillery, as they would throughout the war. In the front-line zone, they had approximately 33,000 guns, but unfortunately, they lacked the vehicles needed to tow them. In the mobile battle to come, these guns were often captured or destroyed by the Red Army to prevent them from being used by the rapidly moving Germans.

What may come as a surprise to some of you reading this is the strength of the Soviet armored forces. The Red Army possessed a staggering number of tanks at the beginning of the war, and some of them were quite good—actually, two models, in particular, were perhaps the best in the world for a short time. We will discuss the T-34 and the KV series shortly, but for the most part, the numbers of the Soviet armored forces were boosted by a tremendous number of armored cars and obsolete and somewhat experimental tanks.

The BT-10 was a lightly armored car designed as a scout/recon vehicle and for urban/crowd control whose armor was just over half an inch at its thickest. Though it mounted a 45 mm gun, which was a heavy caliber for its chassis, the vehicle was useless on the battlefield unless it was against unescorted infantry with no anti-tank weapons.

Then came a series of light and medium tanks, most of which had been designed in the mid-1930s. Thousands of T-27s and T-28s were built and used in the Soviet invasion of eastern Poland. There, they proved somewhat effective, as most of the quality Polish units had moved west to fight the Nazis. However, in the Winter War against the Finns, the Soviet tanks were found to be vulnerable to anti-tank fire and Molotov cocktails, flammable liquid bombs used by the Finns to make up for their lack of anti-tank guns. It didn't help that the Soviets thought their tanks would be suited perfectly to fight in the war against the Finns. Near the start of World War II, the Soviets up-armored these tanks, which helped to a degree. Another factor that deluded the Soviets into thinking their tanks were capable was their victory over the Japanese in Mongolia, where the Japanese provoked an "incident" that led to a large battle at Khalkhin Gol. This was deceptive, however, for, among all of the major combatants of WWII, the Japanese tanks were the worst.

There was also the T-35 "land battleship," which was more in line with WWI-thinking than WWII. The T-35 was a huge machine with multiple turrets and a crew of eleven. Its heaviest gun was a good 76.2 model combined with a host of machine guns and two 45 mm guns. Its top speed, which could only be rarely used for its use of fuel, was 19 miles per hour. The tank was almost 32 feet long and weighed 44 tons, making it liable to sink in the mud and almost impossible to get over most of the primitive bridges in the Soviet countryside. Plenty of pictures exist of German soldiers examining this oddity on the battlefield after they had been knocked out or abandoned.

Illustration 2: German soldiers pose on T-35, fall 1941

The Soviets had also purchased a number of British tanks before the war, but most of these were obsolete by the time World War II began.

However, the Red Army began turning out two excellent tank models beginning in 1940. These were the Kliment Voroshilov (named for the Soviet marshal of the same name) 1 and 2. The KV-2 is the more well-known of the two, with its huge profile and awkward-looking and heavily armored turret, but the KV-1 was a beast itself and proved to be a challenge for the Germans when they met it on the battlefield.

The KV-1 sported 90 mm front armor with 75 mm sides and 70 mm rear armor—in other words, it was a well-protected tank. It carried an excellent 76.2 mm main gun, which was heavier than all German tank guns at the time of Operation Barbarossa, and three to four 7.62 mm machine guns. Its tracks were wider than previous Soviet tanks, which allowed it, and the more famous T-34, to operate in mud and snow much more successfully than other Soviet and German tanks. The height of the KV-1 was just over eight feet, or twelve feet if one includes the turret.

The KV-2 was almost sixteen feet high including its turret, but its turret and front armor were (or approached) 110 mm/4.3 inches. Its main gun was an artillery gun of 152 mm/5.9 inches (its main purpose was mobile artillery). Its main weakness, though, was its lack of speed, although its armor somewhat made up for this.

Both versions of the KV tanks proved to be a shock to the Germans and Finns on the field, and many German battlefield reports and diaries, such as the one below, which comes from a soldier in the 1st Panzer Division on the second day of the invasion, are filled with accounts of how much damage these vehicles could take.

Our companies opened fire from 700 m (765 yd). We got closer and closer... Soon we were only about 50-100 m (55-110 yd) from each other. A fantastic engagement opened up—without any German progress. The Soviet tanks continued their advance and our armor-piercing projectiles simply bounced off. The Soviet tanks withstood point-blank fire from both our 50 mm (1.97 in) and 75 mm (2.95 in) guns. A KV-2 was hit more than 70 times and not a single round penetrated. A very few Soviet tanks were immobilized and eventually destroyed as we managed to shoot at their tracks, and then brought up artillery to hammer them at close range. It was then attacked at close range with satchel charges.

Until the Germans began to field their 88 mm anti-aircraft guns as an anti-tank weapon, the best that the German gunners could hope for was a lucky hit on a faulty area of armor or to disable the tank by hitting its tracks. In close-combat situations, satchel charges (as mentioned above) might disable the tank, but that took extraordinary courage.

Lastly, the Soviets developed the ground-breaking T-34. Seeing the success of lighter German tanks in Poland, France, and the Low Countries in 1940, the Soviets rushed plans that were already on the drawing board to the production line. The result was the T-34/40. "T" stood for "tank," "34" for the year that designer Mikhail Koshkin had developed his idea for the tank, and "40" for the year it entered production. Later versions were called T-34/76 and 85, but they were not by the Soviets; this was a German name for tanks with those gun sizes.

The T-34 was honestly not a great tank. It was just a very good one, and it was very good at nearly everything. It had speeds of 53 km/33 mph. Its gun was a high velocity 76 mm gun, capable of penetrating all German tanks in 1941 at a distance. Its wide tracks allowed it to move well in muddy or wet soil, and it was not too heavy for most serious bridges. Its diesel engine was simple, reliable (which the KVs were not), and easy to repair. The profile of the tank was not too high, and best of all, it used cast armor in most places as opposed to the riveted armor used on most tanks in most countries of that time.

Cast armor meant that large sections of the tank's armor were made in one piece. Where the pieces met, they were welded together rather than riveted, making them much stronger. Additionally, rivets had a nasty habit of being jarred loose by anti-tank rounds, turning them into large chunks of shrapnel flying inside the tank, even if the shell did not penetrate it.

The armor itself was sloped, which was yet another innovation. This meant that added strength was given to the armor, as a round would actually have to penetrate further on sloped armor, which had the same thickness as non-sloped armor. Sloping also meant that anti-tank rounds were often deflected upward rather than penetrating the tank. Though the T-34's armor was not as thick as that of the KV series, early WWII German tank and anti-tank guns often could not penetrate the outer hull of the T-34, especially at a distance. Captured T-34s were carefully examined by the Germans, and as a result, and with some modifications, the Panzer Mark V Panther was developed.

German Tanks

In the years between World War I and World War II, the Germans had also been working on new tank designs. Though the Treaty of Versailles forbade Germany to possess anything except lightly protected armored cars for riot/crowd control duty, some generals and other officers, both those on active duty and those forced into civilian life by the treaty, constantly worked for the day that Germany would be able to rearm.

By 1929/30, when the Great Depression was at the forefront of the minds of the great powers of the West, and after more than a decade had passed since World War I, the Allied observation of the German military had become lax. Many in Britain and the United States (and, to a lesser degree, France) had come to believe that the terms of the Treaty of Versailles weighed too heavily on Germany. Also, at a time when capitalism seemed to be under threat, the Allies were well aware that Stalin and his communist allies in Europe were waiting for their moment to seize power. As Germany was the only nation able to take on the Soviet Union in that area of the world, many British and Americans began to see a renewed German Army as a bulwark against communism, and so, they often looked the other way as the Germans made plans to rearm.

Interestingly enough, much of their planning took place away from the prying eyes of the Allies: it took place in the Soviet Union, as was mentioned earlier. However, these secret training bases were focused more on training pilots and developing an air force, something which concerned the British and Americans, as fighters and bombers weren't hindered by the sea like tanks and machine guns.

German tank planning and engineering took place on private drawing boards throughout the country. A small number of German troops practiced tank warfare with plywood and cardboard cutouts that they carried as they ran around training fields. Western newsreel cameras made fun of this, but many of the men running about would become the same tank commanders that were the spearhead of the blitzkrieg ("lightning war") tactics, which overwhelmed most of Europe in 1939 and 1940. Despite its comical appearance, this training went a long way toward learning a new type of tank warfare in which the tank became its own devastating weapon, driving deep behind enemy lines in large, powerful armored columns rather than in small infantry-support groups where their firepower and maneuverability were effectively reduced.

When the Germans invaded the USSR in June 1941, they did so with an estimated 6,000 armored vehicles. The bulk of the German tanks were Panzer Mark Is and IIs, both of which were obsolete even before the war began in Poland in 1939. The Mark I was more of a turreted armored car than a tank, though it had treads. Its armor was thin and riveted, and it was armed with only two 7.92 mm machine guns, which were mounted in the turret. It had no cannons whatsoever. The vehicle was good for putting down lightly armed civil insurrections, and that was about it. Its thickest armor was half an inch thick, and that was just in the front. The tank was susceptible to even the smallest caliber anti-tank guns. As the war went on, the thousands of Mark Is were gradually modified; many of them had their turrets removed, and their chassis were able to carry a variety of guns as "tank destroyers" and mobile artillery.

The Panzer Mark II was a slight improvement. German military observers and intelligence agents in other countries, particularly France, reported that many of the tanks they were seeing were significantly better than the Germans. The Germans began a crash course in building better tanks, but as a stopgap, they constructed the Mark II, which was made by the same factories that made the Mark I. The most significant difference between the two tanks was the 20 mm/2 cm guns the Mark II carried as opposed to the machine guns of the Mark I. The Mark II also had a hull-mounted 7.92 mm machine gun for defense against infantry. The tank could easily be destroyed by most Allied anti-tank guns.

As the Mark Is and IIs were making their way through Poland, German engineers were busy designing an up-to-date tank for the *Wehrmacht*. This was the Mark III, which became the workhorse of the German Army, going through a number of modifications (mostly increases in armor protection and larger, longer cannon) throughout the conflict. A total of nearly 6,000 Mark III variants were built in 1943, and many of the survivors saw duty in various Eastern European countries after the war.

So, if the German tanks were actually not as good as many of the Allied tanks they faced, particularly at the start of the war, why do we consider the Germans the masters of armored warfare during World War II? Well, war is more than just equipment: it's also about training, leadership, discipline, and tactics.

But what were the tactics that allowed the Germans to surprise and overwhelm their enemies in the first two years of the war? Broken down to its most basic form, the blitzkrieg consisted of a variety of elements all working together. Firstly, weak points in the enemy's defenses would be found. Strong points would be avoided, maneuvered around, or simply held in place by a feinting attack. Then, a strong armored column, working in close conjunction with massive concentrated air attacks, would drive through the weak points of the enemy's front, penetrating to the rear to cut off supplies, interrupt communication, and sow confusion. German infantry would then drive through the hole broken open by the tanks and air support to mop up and surround enemy units still at the front.

On many occasions, especially in the more open fields of Poland and Russia, tank formations would keep driving until they reached their goals or were in danger of
outrunning their supply trains.

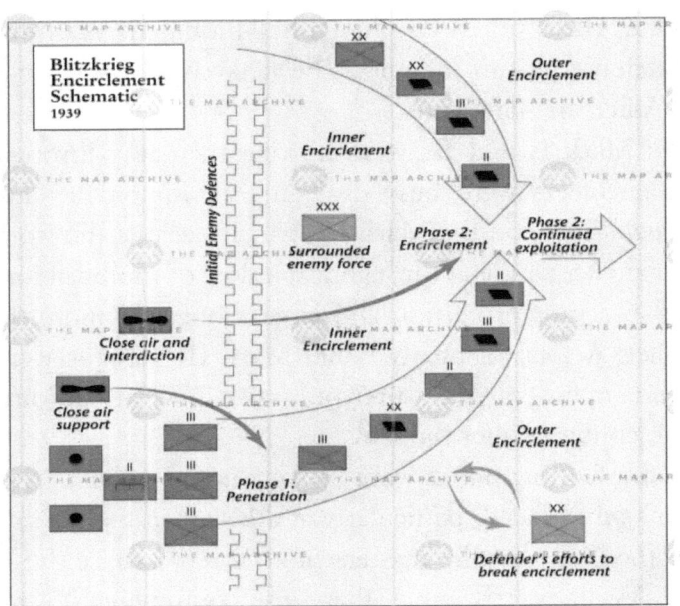

Illustration 3: Diagram of theoretical blitzkrieg-type breakthrough of WWII (courtesy The Map Archive)

German tactics also called for the use of airpower acting in close coordination with armored and infantry units on the ground. This called for a high level of skill that the Soviets did not possess at this point. Adding to the strength of the German attack was their complete superiority in the air. Though the Soviets possessed many more planes than the Nazis, the vast majority were obsolete when the war began, and many of those were in a state of disrepair. Later in the war, the Soviets fielded a number of decent fighters and dive bombers (especially the famed Ilyushin Il-2 dive bomber, which was the scourge of German tank formations later in the war), but almost until the day the war ended, the German kills of Soviet aircraft were much, much higher than Soviet destruction of German planes.

The Soviets had seen the German tactics at work in Poland in 1939 and in the West in the summer of 1940, but in the summer of 1941, they still did not have an effective counter to German battlefield tactics. They hoped that their troops in Poland would be able to hold them back at least long enough for the complete mobilization of the Red Army and that the weight of Soviet equipment and manpower would be able to grind the Germans down.

Chapter 2 – Invasion

On the night of June 21st, 1941, a German soldier named Alfred Liskow, who had been a member of the Communist Party of Germany before Hitler, swam across the Bug River in Poland and defected to the Soviets. He warned them that the German Army was under orders to attack the Soviets the next morning. The warning went unheeded, though a few weeks later, Liskow allegedly broadcast propaganda to the Soviet people that many Germans did not want a fight with the Soviet Union. His fate is unclear, although he was likely executed on Stalin's orders in 1942.

Many warnings about Hitler's intentions went unheeded by Stalin. Flights by German planes, which were clearly reconnaissance planes, were ordered to be left unmolested by Stalin as he did not want to provoke an "incident," as he believed the Red Army was unready for a fight. His military intelligence staff warned him an attack was imminent, and so did many of his generals, who were clearly taking their lives in their hands to do so. Even Winston Churchill, who was privy to much of Germany's thinking and actions through his intelligence and code-breaking services, warned the Soviets that an invasion was coming—and soon. Stalin ignored Churchill, believing the Englishman to be attempting to provoke him into attacking Germany and taking the pressure off Britain.

But perhaps most significantly, Stalin ignored reports from one of his agents in Japan, Richard Sorge, who was privy to information from diplomatic circles in Tokyo. Sorge reported in late May that he believed Hitler would attack the USSR in late June. He learned this from a German officer in Tokyo that he had befriended. Sorge was also sleeping with the German officer's wife, and she provided him with additional intelligence. All of this information he sent to Moscow, which was ignored. Fortunately for the Soviets, Stalin believed Sorge in late 1941 when Sorge informed Moscow that Japan had no intention of attacking the USSR and would go to war with the US instead, allowing Stalin to bring massive numbers of men and materials west from the Russian Far East to fight the Nazis at the gates of Moscow.

Sorge, among other spies and intelligence officials, Churchill, and Alfred Liskow were right: on June 21st, German commanders received the message that Unternehmen (Undertaking/Operation) Barbarossa would begin the next morning. The operation was named after medieval German Holy Roman Emperor Friedrich Barbarossa (Frederick I, "Red Beard"), who is, according to legend, not dead but just sleeping, ready to awake and lead Germany to greatness in its hour of need.

Just after 3 a.m., thousands of German guns opened fire along an 1,800-mile-long front, which was, at the time, the largest artillery barrage in history, though that would be surpassed many times over during the war. Three million German troops and their allies poured over the borders in Poland, the Baltic states, Ukraine, and in the north bordering Finland. Though Soviet units had been sent an alert two hours before, word was slow getting to them, if it got there at all, and virtually none of the Red Army formations at the front was ready for the German onslaught.

The German fighter planes attacked Soviet airbases near the front line, destroying much of the Soviet air forces on the ground. German bombers attacked targets all along the border and deep into the

USSR, striking targets as far as the Leningrad suburbs and Odesa in Ukraine.

In Moscow, Josef Stalin was completely destroyed by the news of the German attack. For a man as paranoid as the Soviet leader, it seems he believed that Hitler would not attack, at least not for the foreseeable future. Stalin went into a deep depression, which lasted for a number of days, and at one point, he believed that he might be arrested by his secret police and/or military for underestimating the threat Hitler posed. That morning, Soviet Foreign Minister Vyacheslav Molotov went on the air and attempted to rally the Soviet people, as Stalin was incapable of speaking. Stalin did not go on the air until July 3rd, which was when he announced the start of the Great Patriotic War. He also slowly began to open churches and bring back previously forbidden military symbols (like the gold braid) and other old traditions in an effort to rally the people and make the war less about communism and more about national survival.

In a way, Stalin was right. World War II in the Soviet Union, as well as Poland, was the most savage war the world had seen since the Mongol invasions of the 13th and 14th centuries. Hitler told those in his inner circle that the war against the Soviet Union was to be a "war of annihilation," eliminating not just the communist system (which, among other things, championed the unity of all the working classes, regardless of race) but also the entire population of the Soviet Union, especially the Jews, of which there was an estimated five million. The Slavic people of the Soviet Union were to be starved or worked to death for the benefit of the Germans. Those permitted to exist were to be kept purposefully ignorant and barely alive to prevent uprisings.

On the heels of the invading troops, echelons of the *Schutzstaffel* (SS) and police units called *Einsatzgruppen* or "special action groups" fanned out to round up and/or kill Jews, Communist Party officials, the intelligentsia (writers, teachers, journalists, etc.), and others deemed a danger by the Nazis. Of course, the Jewish community was the primary target, and a year before the first extermination camps were organized, the *Einsatzgruppen* killed an estimated 1.5 million people in what has been recently termed the "Holocaust by bullets."

In just weeks, the Germans had penetrated hundreds of miles into the Soviet Union. Poland and the Baltic states of Latvia, Lithuania, and Estonia were taken in days, and by July 2nd, the Germans were at the Stalin Line, a line of defenses outside Leningrad. Hitler, Joseph Goebbels, Heinrich Himmler, and others down the chain of Nazi command were, given the extent of German successes in the summer of 1941, exultant and prepared plans for the German colonization of the Soviet Union from Archangelsk in the far north to the Ural Mountains to the Caspian Sea.

Indeed, in the first few weeks, it appeared as if the Red Army would either be eliminated in the field, taken prisoner, or disintegrate. Huge pockets of Soviet troops were surrounded in what historians have termed "the great encirclement battles of 1941." The blitzkrieg worked amazingly well, just as it had in the West.

In battles both large and small, Soviet units were encircled and destroyed. Though conventional military theory says that an attacker should enjoy at least a two to one advantage, the attacker does have the advantage of deciding where to attack, and in keeping with blitzkrieg tactics, the Germans, generally speaking, pushed their armored spearheads against areas of the Soviet lines that were less well-defended, had gaps in the lines, or were manned by less able, less equipped, or poorly trained troops, or some combination of the three. Two prongs of the German forces would meet after penetrating miles behind Soviet front-line troops, completing an encirclement of the Red Army forces. Sometimes, a double envelopment, or a pincer movement, would occur, in which elements of the German forces would continue to drive on, hoping to then catch reinforcing Soviet units in another encirclement.

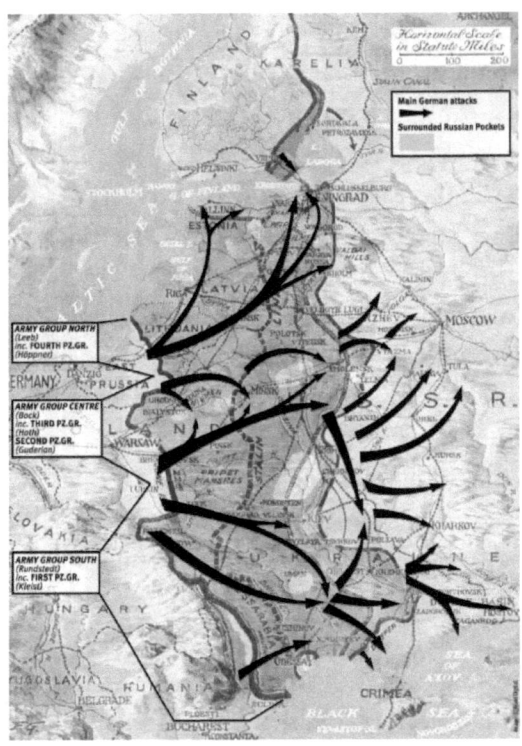

Illustration 4: German advances in December 1941

As you can see on the map above, these encirclements happened on both a small scale and a large one. If you look at the thrust of Germany's "Army Group Centre," you will see a series of arrows hundreds of miles apart coming together after driving deep into Soviet territory. On a smaller unit scale, this happened hundreds of times.

Initially, the Soviets were not only hampered by the Germans' tactics and power, especially in the air, but also by the instructions they were getting from Moscow. Because of the purges, Soviet officers were loath to take initiative: if they made the wrong choices, they might end up before a firing squad. Sometimes, the instructions battlefield commanders did receive were so out of touch or out of date that they were irrelevant to what the commanders were facing. Delays caused by German interruptions to Soviet communications, hesitation on the part of Soviet soldiers up and down the chain of command to relay bad news, and indecision at the top made a coordinated Red Army response almost impossible.

In the initial hours of the invasion, Stalin issued an order for Soviet troops to counterattack wherever possible, and that was essentially the gist of the order—no specifics were given, and no coordination between units happened. Commanders were simply ordered to attack whatever Germans they could with whatever troops they had. Knowing that a firing squad was virtually assured for anyone who disobeyed orders, hundreds of fruitless and fatal Soviet attacks took place. These battles were more like a boxing match in which one of the contestants is the heavyweight champ while the other is some guy off the street.

Panic spread throughout the country. People near the front lines attempted to flee, but on many occasions, they found themselves surrounded like the Red Army troops that were supposed to defend them. Columns full of thousands of people were bombed by the German Air Force, the *Luftwaffe*.

On the southern part of the front, in Ukraine, the Germans were often welcomed as liberators. Many older Ukrainians remembered the German occupation of World War I, in which the Germans acted with restraint and even respect. Others in the country had a deep abiding hatred of Stalin and the Soviet system, which had ruthlessly suppressed Ukrainian nationalism during and after the Russian Civil War, which took place between 1918 and 1921. Worse still, Stalin had deliberately deprived Ukraine of food during the years of 1932 and 1933, resulting in a man-made famine that was only aided by a natural disaster, which killed at least a million people in Ukraine, most of them ethnic Ukrainians. Of course, many hundreds of thousands of Ukrainians fought against the German invasion, but throughout the country, mobs greeted the invading German troops with the traditional gifts of welcome—bread and salt—and garlanded them with flowers.

This welcome by the Ukrainians encouraged the Nazis to believe that it was only a short matter of time before the Soviet system, under pressure from the outside and hopefully soon from within, would fall apart. However, if Hitler had chosen to look more deeply, especially as June faded into late July and August, he might have recognized that this fight was going to be more difficult than he imagined.

First, whatever goodwill existed in Ukraine, as well as the Baltic states, where the hatred of Russia ran deep, soon disappeared when the Nazis showed themselves to be, well, Nazis. By the fall of 1941, the kernels of organized resistance had begun to grow, and by 1942, it would grow to be well-organized and increasingly well-equipped, not to mention numerous.

Second, the Germans, though they had inflicted immense casualties on the Soviets, were also suffering huge losses, and unlike the Soviets, they could ill afford them. And not only did their losses mount, but supplies also began to run short. The Germans did not plan for a protracted war, and their resources of oil, metals, and the other things needed for a protracted conflict began to run out. This would only get worse with time. And, of course, the distances involved also made it difficult for the Germans to get supplies to their front-line troops, especially with the arrival of bad weather and the increasing numbers of partisans as the war continued.

Third, Soviet resistance began to stiffen as the months dragged on. Diaries kept by German soldiers in the field speak of the fanatic resistance of some Soviet troops, which increased the farther the Germans drove into the country, as the Soviets began to realize more and more that this war was one not just of conquest but also of annihilation.

As summer turned into fall, and then fall into winter, the Red Army began to show itself more capable. Part of this was due to the weather, but as time went by (and especially by the second half of the war), Stalin smartly realized that he was not the military genius he had thought himself to be on June 21st, 1941. Where Hitler increasingly took control away from his generals, Stalin gave them more leeway. This meant that Soviet troops in many, but not all, circumstances could retreat to fight another day and that his field commanders had a greater say in where and when to attack and retreat, as well as in the allocation of troops and supplies. As we will see, better-trained Soviet Far Eastern troops arrived near Moscow in late November/early December 1941, once Stalin realized the Japanese were attacking across the Pacific. Additionally, the Soviets began a more modern training regimen, especially among their generals and mid-level commanders, giving them instruction on combined arms attacks. By the second half of 1943, the Soviets were masters of the blitzkrieg themselves.

Lastly, though it took some time before it could have an effect, both Great Britain and the United States began sending massive amounts of military support and other aid to the Soviet Union. Though most Soviet tanks and planes were made at home, the Western Allies shipped tens of thousands of trucks, rifles, machine guns, food supplies, ball bearings, and factory parts to the USSR, even while they were fighting the Germans themselves. Both British Prime Minister Winston Churchill and US President Franklin Delano Roosevelt knew that should the Soviet Union be defeated or come to terms with Hitler, the war in Western Europe would be over, or, at the very least, the victory would be greatly delayed and come at a much higher cost.

Chapter 3 – All Seems Lost

In the months before Operation Barbarossa, Hitler and many of the leading figures on his general staff debated what the main goal of the operation would be. Many people have a vision of Hitler as a raving madman, ranting and threatening his generals until he got his way. This certainly was the case many times in the latter part of the war. However, in the first part of the conflict, he was more likely to listen and debate with his officers, and this is what happened in the lead-up to the invasion of Russia.

World War II spawned an entire industry—alternative history. Pages upon pages have been written on "how and if Hitler could have won WWII," and many of them focus on his actions, or lack of them, in the Soviet Union, and to be sure, what follows here will be debated by those who read it.

Very generally speaking, Hitler's plan was to knock the Soviets out of the war by capturing what he believed to be the most important part of the country—the south. There, Ukraine supplied the majority of grain and other foodstuffs to the people of the USSR. It also contained vast supplies of coal. Farther east in the south were the oil fields of the Caucasus, which were some of the richest in the world, especially those in Baku, and if there was one key resource the German war machine lacked, it was oil.

Hitler also believed an attack to the north would liberate the Baltic nations from communism, and this liberation, carried to its fullest extent, would reach the port of Murmansk, where the Soviet Union had its western port. Taking Murmansk would help in cutting off any possible supplies brought in from Britain or elsewhere. The capture of Leningrad would also dishearten the Soviets as it was the "home" of their revolution. Perhaps most importantly, Hitler and some of his supporters in the military believed that the most important factor would be the destruction of the Red Army in the field, preferably in the vast plains between Poland and Moscow.

However, many of Hitler's leading generals, especially General Erich Marcks, believed that the best strategy would be to utilize the majority of the German strength and make a drive toward Moscow, "cutting off the head of the snake," as one of them put it. With their capital taken and their armies demoralized in the field, the Soviets would either sue for peace or fall apart.

The Balkans

Before Hitler and his generals could prove or disprove each other's theories, they were faced with a situation that completely threw off their timetable. Hitler's plan was to invade the USSR in mid-May. This would give the German forces perhaps six months of good weather before the Russian winter set in. They were confident (one could easily say over-confident) that they could achieve their goals in that time, and despite the delay described to you below, they continued to believe Operation Barbarossa would be over before the worst of the weather hit.

In October 1940, Benito Mussolini, the fascist dictator of Italy and Hitler's ally, invaded Greece without telling Hitler of his plans. Mussolini was sure his armies would be in Athens in a short period of time, and then he would be able to brag of yet another addition to his "New Roman Empire" of Albania, Libya, Ethiopia, and a small sliver of southern France that had been given to him as a gift by Hitler after the defeat of that country. Mussolini's plans went completely awry, with the Greeks not only mounting a stout defense but also counterattacking and driving the Italians back into Albania where their attack began.

Soon, it became clear to Hitler that he would have to bail out his Italian friend lest the British use Greece as a base of operations against his own southern flank, and so, Germany was rushing troops to Greece as fast as possible.

But in order for German troops to get to Greece, they needed passage through Yugoslavia. The regent of Yugoslavia, Prince Paul, who was holding the throne for the future king, Peter II, to come of age, was pro-German and was prepared to let the German troops pass through the country. Anti-German forces, alarmed at this loss of national sovereignty and the possibility that German troops might not leave, staged a coup and placed Peter II, who was pro-Ally in his outlook, on the throne. Peter II and his generals refused Hitler's troops passage just days before their planned movement south.

So, on April 6th, 1940, Hitler and Mussolini invaded Yugoslavia from the south and north, and though they fought hard, the Yugoslavs were overwhelmed in two weeks. The German troops moved south at the same time and conquered Greece by April 30th. A month-long campaign to take the large island of Crete then ensued, but by the start of June, all of Greece was under Axis control.

Though the operations in the Balkans was relatively quick, it pushed back Hitler's invasion of the Soviet Union by about six weeks. Many historians have argued that these six weeks were crucial in allowing the Soviets to regroup in the fall and for the Russian winter to set in, as the Germans only approached Moscow in late October/early November 1941. However, some believe that in the long run, even if the Germans had captured Moscow, the Soviets would have fought on, having already moved most of their industrial plants to the Ural Mountains in one of the most amazing feats of reorganization in modern history. At Stalin's order, virtually every vital factory part and machine, not to mention supplies and manpower, were removed before the Germans arrived and moved hundreds of miles to the east, out of range of the German bombers. That which could not be moved was simply destroyed.

Back to Russia

The first part of the Great Patriotic War was a series of great encirclement battles fought on the western Russian and Ukrainian plains. These types of actions were fought throughout the early German campaign, and a number of these larger battles took place, in which hundreds of thousands of men were involved (and sometimes, in the case of the Red Army, were taken as prisoners).

The first major battle of Operation Barbarossa took place in the region near the Polish city of Bialystok and the Soviet city of Minsk, which were about 215 miles apart. The battle started on the opening day of the invasion, June 22nd, and lasted until July 9th. The German *Wehrmacht* used the blitzkrieg and envelopment tactics described earlier to surround, kill, and capture a large number of Soviet troops, who were trapped in the area by the fast-moving German columns that had them surrounded before they were even aware of it. As a result, nearly half a million Soviet troops were killed, captured, or wounded, 5,000 vehicles destroyed, and almost 2,000 aircraft destroyed, mostly on the ground. This first major battle of the Nazi invasion had many in Germany believing that their thoughts of a quick and relatively easy victory would come true. Compared to the Soviet losses, the Germans lost perhaps 15,000, which included killed, wounded, and missing men.

To the south, another encirclement battle took place, beginning on July 15th and ending on August 8th, near the city of Uman, Ukraine, which led to the most important Ukrainian city, Kyiv (Ukraine's capital today). There, three German Army groups, totaling an estimated 400,000 men and 600 tanks, outmaneuvered three Soviet army groups that totaled 300,000 men, killing or capturing two-thirds of the Soviet force.

The Germans continued to drive eastward, and between July 8th and the end of the month, they engaged the Red Army in a massive battle near the city of Minsk (today the capital of Belarus). Nearly a million men on both sides took part in the battle, each with about the same number of tanks and guns, but yet again, the Soviets were outmaneuvered and surrounded. The Soviet losses were staggering: over 300,000 killed or captured, with 5,000 tanks and 2,000 aircraft destroyed.

As the summer wore on, the Germans were both elated and amazed. They could not believe their good fortune of winning battle after battle and destroying or capturing so many Soviet troops. But how many Soviet troops were there? As the summer turned to fall, the German estimates of Soviet strength proved wrong time and time again. Just when the Germans thought the Russians were finished, new units would turn up at the front.

What's more, even though some of these units had barely any training, and many were put into the front lines with few bullets for their guns or even no guns at all (they were told to get one from the dead on the field), Soviet resistance seemed to stiffen the farther eastward the Nazis drove. At times, it was fanatical, with waves of Soviet soldiers simply charging en masse into German formations. Of course, many times these soldiers had no choice; they would have been killed by the political commissars and troops had they retreated, but it seemed to the Germans that the fighting was getting tougher the farther into Russia they got. Without a doubt, many Soviet troops took the other route and simply gave up—, hundreds of thousands of them, in fact. This leads us to another gruesome fact of World War II. Of the millions of Soviet soldiers taken prisoner by the Germans throughout World War II, especially at the beginning, many were simply put in pens and left to die of exposure, thirst, hunger, and disease, which is rife when people are forced together in unsanitary conditions. Hundreds of thousands were simply shot. Millions were sent to German-controlled territory. Some of them were sent to Germany and other places to work in forced labor camps. Many others were sent to the concentration camps that were sprouting up all over Poland. The first people gassed at Auschwitz were actually Soviet POWs. Making this situation even more tragic is the fact that those who survived the Nazis were often sent to the Soviet Gulag after the war, as Stalin viewed them as potential Western spies and/or traitors for having been captured. Many perished in the Soviet camps after surviving the terrors of the Nazis.

Illustration 5: Masses of Soviet POWs taken in one of the encirclement battles during the first weeks of Barbarossa. Most Soviet POWs would not survive.

As they approached the Soviet capital of Moscow and the Ukrainian city of Kyiv, the Germans fought the Red Army in two more giant encirclement battles: one at Smolensk, located on the approaches to Moscow, during most of July and the other at Kyiv itself from August 23rd to September 26th.

At Smolensk, 430,000 Germans took on over half a million Soviets. The battle took place over an area hundreds of square miles, with thrust and counter-thrust actions occurring throughout the month of July. It even included savage house-to-house fighting in cities throughout the area, especially in Smolensk itself. Throughout the area, atrocities took place on both sides, though the Germans targeted not only the soldiers of the Red Army but also civilians and, of course, the large Jewish population that lived in the area.

Smolensk resulted in another Soviet defeat, with almost 200,000 dead, another quarter of a million wounded, and over 300,000 captured. Furthermore, anywhere between 1,500 and 3,000 armored vehicles of all types and almost 1,000 aircraft were destroyed. The Germans lost much less than that—some 30,000 killed and 100,000 wounded—but unlike the Soviets, they could not afford such losses week after week. And the number of German dead was to increase as time went on.

At the beginning of the conflict, Hitler had ordered his generals to focus on the south, where most of the USSR's resources were located. As the summer wore on, his generals convinced him to change the focus of the German attack back toward the center, but after the Battle of Smolensk, Hitler again ordered a shift, convinced that the Russians were on their last legs and would put more emphasis on saving their resources, especially their coal and oil.

In late August through late September, the biggest of the encirclement battles of Operation Barbarossa was fought near Kyiv. There, half a million German, Hungarian, Romanian, and Italian troops fought an increasingly difficult battle against the Red Army. The Soviets initially had about 600,000 men in the area but fed more troops into the battle as September ground on. The battle didn't take place at the city but rather throughout the northwestern part of Ukraine, encompassing thousands of square miles.

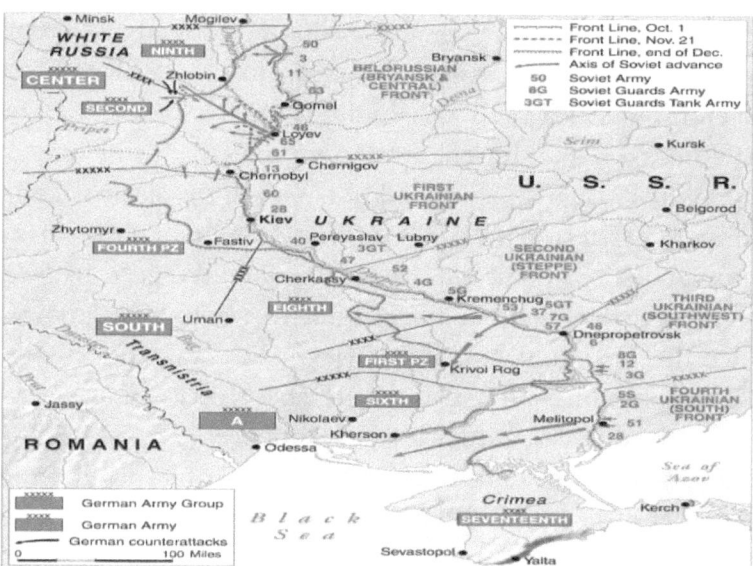

One of the demoralizing effects on the German soldiers was the landscape. Coming from a densely populated country that had many different geographical characteristics, the endless plains of the Soviet Union began to get to them. To many, it was like being at sea or, more accurately, in "a sea of grass," with nothing but rolling hills and the occasional tree or hut to break up the scenery. What's more, the Soviets kept fighting, drawing them farther and farther into this alien landscape.

During the First Battle of Kyiv (Kiev), the Soviets lost hundreds of thousands of men, who were either killed or captured. But the German casualties began to mount, as they had over 125,000 killed, wounded, or missing. Throughout the battles in Ukraine, the Nazi *Einsatzgruppen,* as well as the German Army, committed atrocity after atrocity, the most infamous of which was the slaughter of Jews at Babi Yar on the outskirts of Kyiv. Over 30,000 people were killed (today, the site is a memorial within the city limits). Throughout Ukraine, literally thousands of execution sites have been found since the war's end. If you are interested in learning more about this subject, please take a look at the bibliography for an excellent title on this subject.

In the north, where the country was more wooded and rougher for tanks to traverse, the Germans advanced to the gates of Leningrad. Their Finnish allies agreed to help the Germans by pinning down the Soviet forces on the Karelian Isthmus, much of which had been Finnish until 1940, but they would not assist in the siege of Leningrad. However, they did battle with the Soviets to the north in Karelia, where many ethnic Finns still lived. The 900-day siege of Leningrad will be discussed in an upcoming volume of *Captivating History*.

Once the First Battle of Kyiv (Kiev) was over, Hitler once again shifted the bulk of his forces north to take Moscow, but between the initial shift southward and back again, much time was lost. From the beginning of October until January 1942, the battle raged on in front of the Soviet capital. The German scout troops at one point woke up and were able to see the spires of the Kremlin, but that is as far as the Germans got.

Advised by his spy Richard Sorge in September that Japan would attack westward (and this time believing him, at least partially), Stalin began to move his massive Far Eastern armies westward to defend the capital. On December 7th, 1941, Japan attacked the US at Pearl Harbor, confirming Sorge's reports, and the Soviets then increased the number of troops sent west, all the while having been raising and training millions of more men.

Beginning in October, the weather turned decisively against the Germans. In the fall and spring, western Russia and Ukraine are subject to rains that turn the countryside (and the many dirt roads of the time) into quagmires. Troop and tank movements slowed or ground to a halt completely. When fall began to turn into winter, the roads began to freeze, allowing the German tanks to be able to advance again.

However, it had become abundantly clear that the Germans were ill-prepared for a winter war. As Winston Churchill said in a speech during the war, "there is snow, there is frost and all that. Hitler forgot about the Russian winter. He must have been very loosely educated." German troops faced sub-zero temperatures while wearing summer clothing. Germans at home began to get the idea that something was wrong when they were asked to donate winter clothing, even women's furs, to the soldiers in Russia.

Meanwhile, German supplies dwindled. Gas was running short, and the weather and increasing partisan attacks made the situation worse. Tanks and other machines had to be kept idling all the time, or else they would freeze. Frostbite took thousands off the front lines, sometimes even into shallow graves.

And then, on December 5th, 1941, the Soviets counterattacked. Masses of Soviet soldiers came pouring out of the mist atop T-34 tanks that were not even painted because they were needed *immediately* at the front. They succeeded in pushing the Germans back hundreds of miles from the Soviet capital until the Germans were able to mount a counter-offensive and stabilize the front line. But the danger to the Soviet capital was over, and Moscow would not be threatened again.

Conclusion

Operation Barbarossa was only the first phase of Hitler's plan to conquer the Soviet Union. From a strictly military standpoint, the operation was a success. Millions of Soviet troops had been killed and captured, and tens of thousands of square miles of Soviet territory had been seized.

But, as Hitler was to admit to Finnish Field Marshal Mannerheim in 1942, he and his generals had seriously underestimated the Soviet capacity to wage war. They had misunderstood the industrial plants built by Stalin before the war and did not expect the Soviets to be able to evacuate much of that industry to the Ural Mountains, which was out of the range of his bombers. He also underestimated the willingness of the Soviet people to work for victory.

Given the ease with which Hitler won the first battles of the campaign, it's easy to see how his ideas about Soviet military skills were reinforced, but as the Soviets were being defeated in the first months of the war, they were also learning, and incompetent officers were being replaced by the leaders that would take the Red Army into Berlin in 1945.

And finally, though the Soviets lost far more men to the Germans than the other way around, most of the surviving German soldiers would have told you that the last thing they would have questioned during the war was the courage of the soldiers in the Red Army.

Bibliography

Bullock, Alan. HITLER AND STALIN: PARALLEL LIVES. New York: Vintage, 2019.

Dear, Ian, and Michael R. Foot. THE OXFORD COMPANION TO WORLD WAR II. New York: Oxford University Press, USA, 2001.

Desbois, Father P. THE HOLOCAUST BY BULLETS: A PRIEST'S JOURNEY TO UNCOVER THE TRUTH BEHIND THE MURDER OF 1.5 MILLION JEWS. New York: St. Martin's Press, 2008.

Roberts, Cynthia A. "Planning for War: The Red Army and the Catastrophe of 1941." *Europe-Asia Studies* 47, no. 8 (1995): 1293-326. Accessed May 6, 2020. www.jstor.org/stable/153299.

"Red Army 1941 > WW2 Weapons." WW2 Weapons. Last modified April 27, 2019. https://ww2-weapons.com/red-army-1941/.

Here's another book by Captivating History that you might be interested in

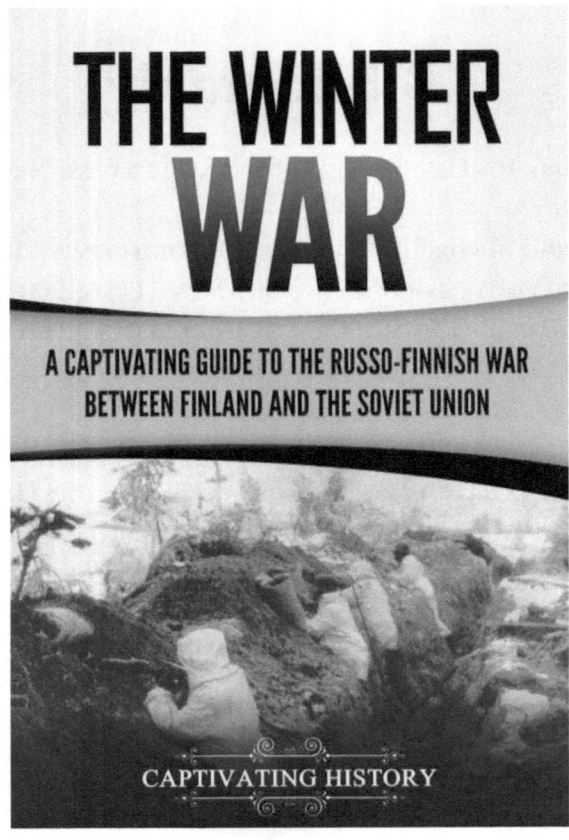

www.ingramcontent.com/pod-product-compliance
Lightning Source LLC
LaVergne TN
LVHW042003060526
838200LV00041B/1854

OPERATION BARBAROSSA

On June 22nd, 1941, Nazi Germany launched Operation Barbarossa, the invasion of the Soviet Union. In the time since the end of the war, the world has become familiar with the number of deaths sustained by the Soviet Union (also known as the USSR) during the conflict—twenty-million. And that's likely low, given the size of the country, census taking at the time, and the damage done to the bureaucracy of the country. Think about it: twenty million people. That is a figure that is almost impossible to wrap one's mind around. Nearly every family in the nation lost someone. The most celebrated and biggest holiday in the Soviet Union, now the nations of Russia, Ukraine, and Belarus (the former Soviet republics that were most affected by the war) is May 8th, "Victory Day, " which celebrates the USSR's victory over Nazi Germany in what was called the Great Patriotic War, honoring the heroes and remembering those lost.

Geoffrey Roberts, a British historian of the Soviet Union in World War II, in his work, Stalin's Wars: From World War to Cold War, 1939-1953 (2006), attempted to tally the losses in terms of infrastructure, making them all the starker. During the Nazi invasion and occupation, the Soviet Union lost an estimated:

About Captivating History

A lot of history books just contain dry facts that will eventually bore the reader. That's why Captivating History was created. Now you can enjoy history books that will mesmerize you. But be careful though, hours can fly by, and before you know it; you're up reading way past bedtime.

Make sure to follow us on Twitter, Facebook and Youtube by searching for Captivating History.

ISBN 978-1-64748-791-1

AUGUSTO

UNA FASCINANTE GUÍA DEL PRIMER EMPERADOR DE ROMA Y DE CÓMO GOBERNÓ EL IMPERIO ROMANO

CAPTIVATING HISTORY